I0210996

IS THERE ANYONE IN AMERICA?

poems by

Pamela Smith

Finishing Line Press
Georgetown, Kentucky

IS THERE ANYONE IN AMERICA?

Publisher: Leah Huete de Maines
Editor: Christen Kincaid
Cover Art: Pamela Smith
Author Photo: Pamela Smith
Cover Design: Elizabeth Maines McCleavy

Order online: www.finishinglinepress.com
also available on amazon.com

Author inquiries and mail orders:
Finishing Line Press
PO Box 1626
Georgetown, Kentucky 40324
USA

Contents

To all those who are perplexed
and to all those who pray

A Note to the Reader

This may come as a challenging, or even strange, read to those who know me as a columnist and a writer of books on biblical, environmental, and historical topics. But the truth is that I never entirely left behind the coffeehouse poet persona that preceded my entrance into a religious community of sisters. Over the years, I've published, among other works, two books of poetry and, now, three chapbooks, along with the occasional poem in a journal.

This collection can be read in one fell swoop, as an answer to the title question: Is There Anyone in America, with the repeated line "Who." Or it can be read as a series of short poems, with each one preceded by that title question. If the poems seem like a cacophony of crazed images, that may well be emblematic of the current state of the nation. Just to clarify a couple of things, though, it may prove helpful to know that some of the allusions come from literature (Whitman), some from lives of saints (Ignatius Loyola, aka Iñigo or Lopez), military installations in South and North Carolina, environmental disasters, justice issues (like the execution by electric chair of an innocent 14-year-old), and social media themes.

Being alive in our times takes patience and invites an attempt to make sense amid what often seems to be mass confusion. That having been said, I offer my thanks to any and all who provide sane and solid refuge. A special note of gratitude goes to the publishers and staff at Finishing Line Press for offering me a third round of publication with them. I'm very grateful, too, to the Weymouth Center for the Arts & Humanities, where I've spent repeated summer stints as one of their writers-in-residence. The first draft of this collection was written there, in Southern Pines, North Carolina, amid the gorgeous gardens and bright mornings which lighten even the darkest nights.

Finally, I offer an Alleluia in honor of everyone and everywhere that the good, the true, and the beautiful persist and prevail.

Is There Anyone in America . . .

Who doesn't have moments of self-doubt

Who doesn't have moments of self-doubt
about what's real and what's artifice or mis-guess,
what's creaturely, what's next door,
when housing in a crowded family cabin
near a lily-padded pool
and waking up, windows cranked open,
only to think that night frogs simply celebrating themselves
with a Whitmaniac "barbaric yawp"
are those in bunks and tight dorms snoring
?

Who really grasps how landscape shapes us,

Who really grasps how landscape shapes us,
which may mean:
saturated in sea water
or super-heated as dust devil and arroyo,
tangled in a bayou with vines and Spanish moss strangling,
or crowded in brick and steel and concrete and crowds and sirens and
sharp whistles and traffic
as one shouldered off to a dank cell by burly captors,
or staring down cliff faces while cleating to climb,
or encircled by dwarf palmettos, brush, lofty pines, live oak, canopies of
leaves,
or ice-skating to music almost in a trance that mixes sweat and chill,
or wheeling across state borders too fast to notice anything
?

Who is harassed by regrets about what they've inherited that isn't largesse or noblesse oblige

Who is harassed by regrets about what they've inherited that isn't
largesse or noblesse oblige
and thinks welcoming the stranger is good—without coyotes and
cages—
and abhors gun violence
and considers the death penalty brutal and a relic of Cro-Magnon or
some such
and would offer Native Americans and African Americans lavish
reparations
and wants a new political party or two
and considers such matters ethical and even religious
and thinks the exploration of inner space is answer and alternative to
outer space
and practically everything else—
no panacea, but progress by ingress
?

Who hasn't tasted the rust-colored sky

Who hasn't tasted the rust-colored sky
and sought to lozenge the throat
and smother a slight cough—
a crush and choke so much like grief—
knowing all the while about far-off wildfires
but trying, trying, trying
not to plot a graph or solve the calculus
of California or Canada or wherever the next Texas-size space burns

or hasn't worried about
what the width and heft of sky-high blanket might portend
?

Who can outroar sonic booms

Who can outroar sonic booms,
the percussion of low jets over Pat Conroy's and Beaufort SC's MCAS
or the pounding like kettle drums from Fort Liberty
or atomic detonations
or skyscraper implosions
or rushes of wildfire
or volcanic bursts of hurricane crush against a seawall—

outroar, that is, the tense and tenor of nature asserting strength and
space
as humans play on somnolently into a danse macabre
without a blink or head snap that wonders—oh yeah—what might be
next

(except or unless a voice on a mighty mountain
keeps insisting, unburned and at unearthly volume, on being itself

and nudging the masses into surrender to mystery)
?

Who can do doodads and katydids

Who can do doodads and katydids
amid Tik-Tok and hip-hop
?

Who might grasp Albert Schweitzer's fellowship

Who might grasp Albert Schweitzer's fellowship—
in time past Gabon—
of those who bear the mark of pain
and, with that prompt, walk now in the shoes of the trafficked in the
USA
one day, two days, three days
and raise a voice, a fist, an outrage
that reaches the ears of sufficient hearts
to stir a single pulse of hope among the sorrowful mothers of
desaparecidos
?

Who considers it worthwhile at times to sit

Who considers it worthwhile at times to sit
amid weeping cherry trees

listening to birds' nocturnes going pianissimo
amid lowering, lowering light
while touching, really touching the shrinking warm

and feeling the music losing itself in long caesura
?

Who not only claims but has integrity

Who not only claims but has integrity—
and is thus steady as sun in timing rise and set,
heedless of clouds,
unconcerned with anyone's admiration,
or whether its coloration flames or pastels,

reliable as the well-maintained downspout
which washes studiously across yard and garden,
even when the rain itself thunders and bubbles and lightnings,
while somehow managing not to flood and toss red mulch into a
spillway
of bloodstain across every cement slab in sight,

steady, reliable, that is, and whole
as clockwork and the sturdy, rooted integers of arithmetic
which are—honestly—only able to be zeroed out
when pitted times an intruding zero
?

Who hasn't played a role at any age

Who hasn't played a role at any age
or every,
shuffling the audience like cards
or spinning like a roulette wheel
without, in the end,
aiming
?

Who, like our friend Santo Iñigo, aka Lopez

Who, like our friend Santo Iñigo, aka Lopez,
has enough discernment to find wonder in
the scent of a baby,
the totter of an elder,
the splay of an osprey nest on a telephone pole,
the plenitude of T-shirts,
the vague attraction of a stale beer smell emitted from the corner bar
and grill,
cook tops, refrigerators, dishwashers,
not to mention elegant pewter tea sets and Keurigs
and coffee mugs all logo-ed up to advertise almost anything,

or
the waterways so dreadfully in need of saving,
pinestraw,
the wit of storytellers and even mourners,
the power of words,
how engineers' minds imagine, then draft and craft,
the shapes of pebbles and shells,

the coffee of consolation,
the wine of desolation—
all before anyone invented the word
jesuitical
?

Who can define and describe Americana accurately

Who can define and describe Americana accurately—
that is, without guile or affrontery
or overdoses of fudging and posing
or hangdog apology
while having to admit to
love-hate relationship
or at least moments of fondness and embarrassment
?

Who hasn't shuddered over newscasts

Who hasn't shuddered over newscasts
that brag they're all local all the time

and wondered, blinkered as service horse or mule,
what we shun and how and why we don't, can't, will not know,
understand, see
?

Who hasn't been caught up in some

Who hasn't been caught up in some
go-carting,
channel-surfing,
lotto-ticket buying,
recreational shopping,
tailgating,
dream chasing,

and ended up slumped over
while clutching tightly
to a whirligig of vicarious whatever
?

Who can give a clear, convincing response

Who can give a clear, convincing response
to the overfed man at the gas pump
who blusters at a woman who has just handed a 20
to a man begging for fuel help:

> "I was trying to signal you.
> That guy's a phony. He's trash.
> He would just as soon shoot you
> and take your car with everything in it.
> See? His plate was from our state, and
> that wasn't his story.
> Coming from far away for a family funeral?
> He's why I carry a gun. I could have shot him.
> Would have, but you were in the way,
> listening, handing him a bill."

or an answer (or affirmation) to the woman, meanwhile,
who, after giving the cash,
hangs back without a word
but notes that the young man, Asian, by the way,
blessed himself, thanked her,
and bought gas
?

Who celebrates those who don't seem to make a New Year's resolution

Who celebrates those who don't seem to make a New Year's resolution
to formulate an updated list of personal and public enemies
?

Who can translate

Who can translate
"Esto vir" into something other than
mustache
and macho

and can imagine that women can be glamorous
in heavier flesh,
in un-stilettoed stance,
in opposition to the eternal reincarnations of Barbie,
women glorying in open air hikes,
dirty shoes, dungarees
?

Who isn't in something for the money

Who isn't in something for the money
and gets the message
(in brusque agreement or sheepishly)
when some pollster says
it's about the economy, stupid
?

Who hasn't snooped and spied into lovetalk

Who hasn't snooped and spied into lovetalk,
bought the scandal sheets that—well, spilled supposed scandal, if not
libel—

or wondered what would come of hidden microphones
or attempts to bug anything smaller than coffee beans
and thus uncover (whether or not with intent to tell)
the secrecies of confessionals or client privileges
?

Who doesn't relish A&E, MTV, BET

Who doesn't relish A&E, MTV, BET,
Magnolia and HGTV, FOX, CNN, Telemundo,
PBS, NPR,
not to mention Netflix, Peacock stream,
and as many flavors of ESPN as Ben and Jerry's ice cream,

all the while tolerating choice-riddled anxiety,
time-ridden loss,
grief over cancellations,
merger and social media renaming distress,
quizzical alphabetics of stations,
with folk, rock, rap, country, soundscapes, classical, whoop-de-do
music-arama in the 100s
hour after hour, day after day,

themselves, we ourselves, unsure if they're/we're
live or reprised
?

Who has mused over whether to learn a language or a dialect

Who has mused over whether to learn a language or a dialect
instead of bellyaching
when overcome
with local, regional, nationwide
polyglottony
?

Who realizes that sometimes while we play

Who realizes that sometimes while we play
hard things happen
and that eyes get tired and burn
not just from too many hours of blue light on screens
or the sometime paperwork of intellectual inquiry
but from the bending backs and tipping heads with endless need
for bandannas or handkerchiefs or rags
to swipe away sweat
?

Who understands that the Carolinas

Who understands that the Carolinas
are more than golf and tourism,

that they include legacy—
in some quarters, of Gullah-Geechee,
of ancestral lands,
of fret over taxes and lack of titles,
of saltwater incursion
where once were fields rife with crops,
of rusted out, tarp-roofed trailers
where plantations long ago stood
on and around what's now named Backache Acres,
?

Who wonders what devils possessed

Who wonders what devils possessed
the ones who battered Emmett Till
or arrested, tried, convicted, and pulled the switch
on 14-year-old George Stinney, Jr.

and what angels made a cause and icon of one
and after 70 years exonerated the other
?

Who doesn't know a bit about the crush of chronic pain

Who doesn't know a bit about the crush of chronic pain
or out-of-nowhere scalding, scathing injury
and so would take the time, we would hope,
to proffer comfort measures, small kindnesses
like cups of chamomile, a pillow,
cooled or warmed-up sheets,
a swirl of water, soft hands soothing a back—
in other words,
let loose our better angels, as Lincoln called them,
himself no stranger to nearly cosmic pain
?

Who, in first response, deals well with blood

Who, in first response, deals well with blood
without dodging into game shows and soaps
like a rocking chair zombie
or a youth soaking up via video
all things fanged and vampired
while claiming he/she/they know(s) it isn't real,
it's simply neat

or, in another vein, deals with blood
without getting paid to donate it
like the sometime drunk (labeled vagrant)
who's seen so much he can only hope his blood
won't, please no, be needed by a buddy
who's suddenly drained of pulse and breath

or deals without squeamishness, denial, or "ick" at first sight
and abrupt removal by excuse,
not knowing that some blood, spilled, can clot and wash
away
without a stain
?

Who might mean it

Who might mean it—
the idea of being a saint,
of living purposefully—when,
on a North Carolina night,
a fixed glance through 10:00 PM trees
appears to be the aurora borealis

even if it's truly an uncanny mix
of shadows, upticks of human light,
cloud and wind and moon

and, knowing that, still seeks beatitude,
besting all that's current
with what's next
?

Who has found

Who has found,
even in the interstices and synapses
of flesh and nerve and bone

that nothing matters

and everything does
?

Pamela Smith, SS.C.M., Ph.D. describes herself as a "binge writer"—which means that she doesn't write every day but that she writes whenever she can wrest time free to sit in a coffee shop and put words on paper or enjoy a stint as a writer-in-residence with notepads and laptop ready for action. She has written hundreds of articles which have appeared in literary and theological magazines, and she appears as a regular columnist and an occasional contributor to the *Catholic Miscellany* and the *Charleston Mercury*.

Her most recent books have been *Holy Wind, Holy Fire, A History of the Diocese of Charleston: State of Grace,* and *How We Can Suffer Our Sorrow and Become Wiser, Better, Gentler People.* Two of her previous chapbooks have been published by Finishing Line: *How Jonathan Green Painted My Momma* (2013) *and Sweet Survival* (2017).

Along with her writing life, she has spent decades as an educator and administrator. Currently she is the ecumenical and interreligious officer of the Catholic Diocese of Charleston and a member of the adjunct faculty in theology for Saint Leo University. She is a member of the Sisters of Saints Cyril and Methodius. After serving in various roles in Pennsylvania, Indiana, and Michigan, she arrived in South Carolina in 2004. The experience of southern life is evident in the short poems of *Is There Anyone in America?*

www.ingramcontent.com/pod-product-compliance
Lightning Source LLC
Chambersburg PA
CBHW022052080426
42734CB00009B/1315